Fun Time with Jesus

Devotional readings for the
beginning reader

Vol. 1

Gloria Trotman, PhD
Karen-Mae Trotman Mitchell, MD, MPH

PRESS

Fun Time with Jesus
Devotional readings for the beginning reader
by Gloria Trotman, PhD, Karen-Mae Trotman Mitchell, MD, MPH

Printed in the United States of America

ISBN 9781613797181

Cover Design: Painting by Eimeliz Garcia
Graphics Consultant: Nelita Elliott PhD

www.xulonpress.com

To

Mom Elsa, who instilled in her children the

personal devotional habit

And

Gabe, Isis, Janae, Joya, Jaselle, Ivan and André

A note to parents and guardians

There are several children's devotional books that are intended for the parent or guardian to read to the children in family devotions. *Fun Time with Jesus* is different. The purpose of this devotional book is to help the child develop a daily **personal** devotional habit from an early age. Young children, who are encouraged to have a few minutes of quiet time alone with God, are better able to develop a personal relationship with Him. They also continue their personal devotional habit throughout their lives. This book is mainly for the child who has just learned to read. However, parents of children ages 0 – 6 will also enjoy reading this book to their children.

Each devotional session is designed to take no longer than five minutes. This includes the THINK/DO assignment. In some cases, the beginning reader may need some help from you. Please be prepared to give all the help and encouragement necessary until the child can go it alone. You will enjoy watching the child grow in love with Jesus, as they meet one on one.

How to Use this Book. Help your child decide on a time and place to have the personal devotional period. It may be in the morning or evening. Your child may choose his or her bedroom, a favorite corner in the house, or even one end of the dining table. Here is where the child and Jesus will meet. Make it special. Also give him/her some pencils, crayons, markers, a notebook and blank paper.

It is our prayer that *Fun Time with Jesus* will be a useful tool in assisting you to help your child build a personal relationship with Jesus.

Success and God's blessings,

Gloria Trotman

Karen-Mae Trotman Mitchell

CONTENTS

PART ONE
Meeting Time

1. Hello, Jesus

2. He Knows My Name

3. His Name Is . . .

4. Holy, Holy, Holy

5. I Will Never Leave You

6. He Picked Me

7. Just Like Me

8. How Many Hairs

9. Talk to Me

10. In His Hand

1. Hello, Jesus

IN MY BIBLE: Let the little children come to me. . . Luke 18:16.

CHAT TIME:

Have you ever met a football player? Sometimes we meet persons we never forget. Can you think of one? How did you feel?

Today, I would like you to meet Jesus. Jesus is the Son of God. He loves boys and girls. Jesus loves you. He is happy to meet you, too. "Hello Jesus!"

DO: How do you like to feel when you meet people? SAD? HAPPY? SCARED? Please circle one word.

PRAYER: Dear Jesus, I am happy to meet You today. Amen.

2. He Knows My Name

IN MY BIBLE: . *I know thee by name.* ***Exodus 33:17***.

CHAT TIME:

Jan did not like to meet Mrs. Sams. Mrs. Sams always forgot her name. Mrs. Sams called her Jane.

"Not Jane, please. My name is Jan."

"Oh, I'm sorry. I just forgot." Mrs. Sams would always say.

Jesus knows your name. He will never forget it.

DO: Write another name that you might like to give yourself. Why would you choose that name?

PRAYER: I thank You, Jesus, that You will always remember my name. Please help me to remember You.

3. His Name Is . . .

IN MY BIBLE: *Thou shalt call his name Jesus for he shall save his people from their sins.* ***Matthew 1: 21***

CHAT TIME:

One of the names of Jesus is *Immanuel*. Another name is *Lord*. Some persons call Him *Christ*. Most persons like to call Him *Jesus.* That name means "Savior." Jesus can save us any time.

Jesus will help you when you need Him. He is waiting to save us even before we call on Him.

DO: Draw a picture of someone saving a pet.

PRAYER: Dear Jesus, I am glad You can save me. Amen.

4. Holy, Holy, Holy

IN MY BIBLE: *You must not use the name of the Lord, your God thoughtlessly.* **Exodus 20:7**

CHAT TIME:

Barb wanted her mother to change her name. Bob's dad thinks he has a funny middle name. So he keeps it a secret. Jesus' name is special. He likes us to call His name. We can call on Him any time.

We can call the name of Jesus when we are praying. We can sing songs about Him. The name Jesus is holy. He is holy like God. My Friend is holy.

DO: Draw a picture of a kid asking Jesus for help.

PRAYER: Dear Jesus, please help me to remember that Your Name is holy. Amen.

5. I Will Never Leave You

IN MY BIBLE: I will not leave you all alone . . . **John 14:18**

CHAT TIME:

My Friend, Jesus, lives in heaven. The Bible says that He can be near me any place I go. That means I am never alone.

Jerry and his friend Mike were riding their bikes. Suddenly, a big black dog started running after them. The boys were afraid. Mike rode faster and faster. Mike left Jerry behind.

Jesus will never leave me alone. When I am scared, Jesus is still with me. Wherever I go, Jesus is with me. Whatever I do, Jesus is with me. What a Friend!

DO: Draw a picture of you and Jesus.

PRAYER: Dear Jesus, I am glad you will be with me even when things get scary. Amen.

6. He Picked Me

IN MY BIBLE: *I chose you. Jeremiah 1:5*

CHAT TIME:

It was recess. The Third Graders were going to play against the Fourth Graders in a big baseball game.

That evening Jimmy was very sad at dinner. Jimmy told Dad that his friends did not choose him to be on the team. "And I so wanted to play," sobbed Jimmy.

"I am sorry that your feelings are hurt, Jimmy," said Mother, putting her arm around him. "Let's talk about it some more." Jimmy told Mother how very sad he was because the kids did not choose him.

Our Bible verse today says, "I chose you." So no matter who thinks we are not cool, that's OK. Jesus will always choose us.

DO: Draw a picture of kids playing together.

PRAYER: Dear Jesus, thank You for choosing me. I would like to choose you too. Amen.

7. Just Like Me

IN MY BIBLE: *And God said, "Let us make human beings in our image and likeness."* **Genesis 1:26**

CHAT TIME:

Raymond and Roger were twins who lived next door to Kay. These eight year-old boys looked exactly alike. Sometimes people got them mixed up. The twins had a lot of fun.

Would you like to look just like your friend? We have a Friend who made us to look like Him.

We do not only want to look like our Friend, Jesus. There are some things we would like to do like Him. We must try to say and do only the things Jesus would. Let us try that today.

DO: Draw a picture of yourself. Now draw a picture of someone you would like to look like.

PRAYER: Dear Jesus, please help me to be just like You. Amen.

8. How Many Hairs?

IN MY BIBLE: *Yes, even God knows how many hairs you have on your head.* ***Luke 12:6***

CHAT TIME:

. . . One hundred thousand one, one hundred thousand two, one hundred thousand three . . . This might be the number of hairs on the heads of some people. Wow! That would take a long time to count.

Jesus knows just how many hairs are on your head? This is because you are very special to Him.

Sometimes we think that we must be like other kids. But Jesus loves us just the way we are. Jesus thinks that we are special. So He came to earth to die for us.

DO: Draw a wig.

PRAYER: Dear God, thank You for making me special. Amen.

9. Talk to Me

IN MY BIBLE: *Evening and morning and at noon will I pray, and he shall hear my voice. Psalm 55: 17*

CHAT TIME:

Chatting can be fun. Bobby likes chatting with Grandma and Grandpa, and his friends.

We must say only kind words when we talk. We should not say words that hurt people's feelings. We should not say things that are not true. Jesus can help us to say kind things.

When we pray to Jesus, we are talking to Him, just like friends do. Jesus likes us to pray to Him.

DO: Write some words you can say that would make Jesus happy?

PRAYER: Dear Jesus, I would like to speak words that would make You happy. Please help me.

10. In His Hand

IN MY BIBLE: *See, I have written your name on my hand. **Isaiah 49:16***

CHAT TIME:

Mr. Jones had tattoos all over his body: on his arms, his legs, and chest. Tattoos were everywhere. Some people get tattoos to help them remember special friends, or special things.

Our Bible verse today says that Jesus has written your name on His hand. Nothing can wash it out. Jesus loves you so much.

So today, say to yourself, "Jesus loves me He is thinking about me all the time."

DO: Draw or write something in your hand. See how long it takes for you to wash it out.

PRAYER: Dear Jesus, Thank you for always remembering me. Amen.

PART TWO
Friendship Time

1. Who Needs a Friend?

IN MY BIBLE: *But a real friend will be more loyal than a brother.* **Proverbs 18:24.**

CHAT TIME

Lisa was scared on her first day at school. The room was full of girls and boys. Mrs. Cox was Lisa's teacher. Lisa sat on a chair near the door. She wanted to cry. Her tummy hurt so badly.

"Please do not cry," said Nancy. "I will sit with you. I will be your friend."

That day, Nancy and Lisa became friends. They had fun playing together. It was a good day.

DO: Draw a picture of someone who has no friends.

PRAYER: Dear Jesus, please help me be a good friend. Amen.

2. Everybody Likes A Friend

IN MY BIBLE: *You are my friends if you do what I command you.* **John 15:14**

CHAT TIME

It is nice to have a friend or two. It is also nice to be a friend, too. The Bible tells us of many things that a good friend will do.

A good friend is kind. A good friend will not hurt you. A good friend is happy when you are happy. If one day you feel sad, your friend will be sorry that you are sad. So we say that a good friend cares about you. We should care about our friends, too.

DO: Do you have a good friend? Draw a picture of that friend.

PRAYER: Dear Jesus, please help my friends to love You. Amen.

3. We Can Share

IN MY BIBLE: *Love your neighbor as you love your-self.* **Leviticus 19:18**

CHAT TIME:

Tommy and his sister Anna were putting their toys away as fast as they could.

"Adam and Becky will be here soon. Those two will not be playing with our toys," said Tommy to Mother who was looking at them.

"Tommy, Anna, are you being selfish? Are you not going to share your toys with Adam and Becky?" asked Mother.

"Perhaps Jesus would not like that, huh," said Anna

"I think you are right," Mother said, "Jesus is happy when we share."

DO: Draw a picture of two friends sharing.

PRAYER: Dear Jesus, please help me not to be selfish. Amen.

4. Friends and Feelings

IN MY BIBLE: . . . *He cares for you.* ***1 Peter 5:7***

CHAT TIME:

"Rex, Rex," Steve called to his dog. Rex did not move. Rex was very sick. Steve was sad all day at school. When Steve got home, Rex was still sick. Steve was still very sad.

Then the doorbell rang. It was Rob. "Hi, Steve! I heard your dog is sick. I came to play with you."

That was very nice. A friend helps us feel better when things are bad.

DO: Make a list of some things you can do to help your friend feel better when he or she is sad?

PRAYER: Dear Jesus, please help me to show love. Amen.

5. A Really Good Friend

IN MY BIBLE: *Trust the Lord with all your heart. Proverbs 3:5*

CHAT TIME:

When we trust a friend, we think that our friend will always be good to us, and will not hurt us.

We trust our family and friends, and our teachers, too. Sometimes we trust persons who look like they are good and kind, but they are not. So we cannot trust everybody. We cannot trust persons who tell lies, and who tell us bad things. We cannot trust persons who hurt us and want to do us bad things. But we have a really good Friend that we can trust—JESUS. He will never hurt us.

THINK: Do you have a really good friend?

PRAYER: Thank you, Jesus, for being my really good Friend. Amen.

6. I Can Trust Jesus

IN MY BIBLE: *So trust the Lord always. Isaiah 26:4*

CHAT TIME

A really good friend will always be kind to us. We say that we can trust that friend. Jesus is a Friend like that. We can trust Him.

Jesus loves us a lot and will not hurt us. Jesus wants only good things for us. He wants us to be happy.

Well, who would not like a friend like that? I like my Friend, Jesus.

DO: Write two things you would like a friend to do for you.

PRAYER: Dear Jesus, I am glad I can trust You. Amen.

7. My Friend's House

IN MY BIBLE: *There are many rooms in my Father's house. John 14:2*

CHAT TIME:

Some persons live in great, big houses called mansions. Other people live in tiny houses.

The other day I saw a house that had 100 rooms. How would you like to live in a house with 100 rooms? Maybe you could have one room full of dolls. Then there could be another room full of trucks. I think one room could be a train room with train tracks all over the floor! Then many trains! Wow!

Our Friend, Jesus, has a big house. Jesus would like you to go there. You can plan for it.

DO: Draw what you think Jesus' house looks like.

PRAYER: Dear Jesus, I would like to be one of the boys and girls at Your house. Please help me. Amen.

8. Come to My House

IN MY BIBLE: . . . *Then I will take you to be with me so that you may be where I am.* **John 14: 3**

CHAT TIME:

Susie did not invite Betty to her party. Betty was sad. Susie said that Betty was not her friend.

Well, we have been invited to the house of Jesus our Friend. Here is what you can do:

Read your Bible to find out what Jesus tells you to do.

Tell Jesus you are sorry when you do things that make Him sad.

Make Jesus your Friend. Jesus can hardly wait for us to go to His house.

DO: Draw a picture of you and Jesus at your house.

PRAYER: Dear Jesus, thank you for Your invitation. Amen.

9. How It All Began

IN MY BIBLE: *For God loved the world so much that He gave His only Son. John 3:16*

CHAT TIME:

A very long time ago, God made Adam and Eve. They lived in a nice, big garden, called Eden. All the things in the garden were for them. They were very happy. God loved them very much.

God told Adam and Eve that they could eat all of the fruits, except the fruit of one tree. If they did, they would die. Satan, a bad angel hated God, Adam, and Eve. Satan told Adam and Eve that they could eat that fruit. So Adam and Eve disobeyed God and ate the fruit God told them not to eat. God was sad.

God told Adam and Eve that they had to leave the garden called Eden. Adam and Eve were sad. But God said He would send Jesus, His Son to earth. Jesus came to die for us.

DO: Draw a pretty garden.

PRAYER: Dear Jesus, please help me to obey You. Amen.

10. Friends Forever

IN MY BIBLE: *I love you . . . with a love that will last forever.* ***Jeremiah 31:3***

CHAT TIME:

"What is that strange red box in your hands, Wendy?"asked Mother.

"My friendship box," said Wendy. "Lily has one, too."

"Friendship boxes,"sneered Tony. "Silly girls."

"That's not silly," said Wendy who was beginning to feel hurt. "Look. Here is a picture of my best friend Lily, and a card she sent me, and a . . ."

"OK, Wendy. What is this box all about?" asked Mother.

"Well, these friendship boxes will make us friends forever," Wendy said.

You have a forever friend, too— JESUS. Yes, He will love you forever.

DO: Put some things in a box to help you think of how much Jesus loves you.

PRAYER: Thank you, Jesus, for your love. I love You. Amen.

PART THREE
Life Time

1. What Do You See?

IN MY BIBLE: *Look! He is coming with the clouds! Every eye will see him.* **Revelation 1:7**

CHAT TIME:

Close your eyes for just a moment, then open them. What was it like with your eyes closed? You could not see at all! You could not see your toys. You could not see your mom's face. You could not see trees outside.

Lots of things are hard to do when we cannot see. It is hard to get dressed. It is hard to write. It is hard to eat.

God gave us many lovely things. He wants us to see them! He wants us to enjoy them. So He gave us eyes. And God promised that one day our eyes will see Him coming back to earth for us!

DO: Close your eyes. Think of something pretty that God made?

PRAYER: Dear Jesus, Thank you for giving me eyes that can see. Amen.

2. What Do You Hear?

IN MY BIBLE: *"…no ear has heard…what God has prepared for those who love him." **1 Corinthians 2:9***

CHAT TIME:

Shhh! Listen. What do you hear?

Grace likes to hear music from her CD. James likes to hear birds sing. Dan likes to hear water splashing at the beach. Ruth likes to hear her brother's voice. Lee likes to hear the doorbell ring. Roy likes to hear Mom play the piano.

What do you like to hear? There are so many great sounds! In Heaven, we will hear angels sing. We will hear Jesus' voice!

God gave us ears to hear. God is so good!

DO: Make a sound that is fun to hear.

PRAYER: Dear Jesus, Please help me to listen to good things. Amen.

3. My Nose Knows

IN MY BIBLE: *If the whole body were an ear, how could it smell? 1 Corinthians* **12:17**

CHAT TIME:

Suppose you did not have a nose!

    Then you could not smell a rose,

    Or fresh bread that Grandma makes,

    Or the cookies that Mom bakes.

    I'm glad that I can smell skunks, too—

    So I can know just what to do.

    When a bad smell comes my way,

    It means that I must stay away!

God really planned me very well

When He made my nose to smell.

THINK: What should you do when you smell smoke? Ask an adult to tell you.

PRAYER: Dear Jesus, Thank you for making me so well! Amen.

4. Raise Your Hand

IN MY BIBLE: . . . *hands that work hard bring wealth to you. **Proverbs 10:4***

CHAT TIME:

Look at your right hand. Touch your thumb to each of your fingers. Lots of animals cannot do that. Dogs cannot do it. Bears cannot do it. Birds cannot do it.

Our hands can do special things that most animals cannot do. We can pick up small things. We can write. We can learn to play music.

Your hands are different from your friend's hands. Your brother or sister does not have hands just like yours. The lines on your hands make your fingerprints. No one else has the same fingerprints you do!

I'm glad my hands can do so many things. Thank You, God!

DO: Trace your hands on a sheet of paper. Cut them out.

PRAYER: Dear Jesus, Thank You for hands that can do so many things. Amen.

5. Let's Jump!

IN MY BIBLE: *How you made me is amazing and wonderful.* ***Psalm 139:14***

CHAT TIME:

Ron was riding his bike one day. He fell and hurt his leg. He had to wear a cast on his leg. It stayed on for many weeks. It was hard for Ron to jump or kick or run. He sat alone at recess. He wished he could play with his friends.

Ron was so happy when his leg was better. He could run again. He could hop. He could jump. He could play with his friends! Ron thanked God for his legs.

DO: Ask an adult to show you a safe place for jumping. Jump as high as you can!

PRAYER: Dear Jesus, Please help my legs to take me to good places. Amen.

6. Mmmm, Mmmm, Good!

IN MY BIBLE: *Taste and see that the Lord is good. Psalm 34:8*

CHAT TIME:

Lee likes big, red grapes. He likes green pears. He likes juicy plums, too! Sometimes, he puts the fruit in the freezer. He likes to eat the cold fruit on hot days. He likes to mix the fruits to make fruit salad. Then he can taste all the yummy flavors!

God gave us many good foods to eat. He gave us taste buds. The taste buds are in little bumps on your tongue. They help us taste all the flavors. We can taste sweet jelly. We can taste salty chips. We can taste sour lemons.

Lee is glad that he can taste food. It makes lunch more fun!

DO: Draw pictures of three fruits that you like.

PRAYER: Dear Jesus, I'm glad I can taste the good food You made. Amen.

7. Just Right

IN MY BIBLE: *God has placed each part in the body just as he wanted it to be. **1 Corinthians 12:18***

CHAT TIME:

Jill's shirt did not feel right. She looked in the mirror. Her shirt was on backwards! That was why it did not fit well. Jill had made a mistake.

Suppose God had put your eyes on your back. How would you see where you were going? What if your legs were stuck together? How would you walk?

God put our body parts together just right. We are glad God does not make mistakes!

DO: Make a person out of play dough or clay.

PRAYER: Dear Jesus, thank you for my body. Amen.

8. Too Many Cookies!

IN MY BIBLE: *So eat and drink and do everything else for the glory of God. 1 Corinthians 10:31*

CHAT TIME

Ann loves cookies. Mom gave Ann two cookies. Ann ate them for dessert. They were so tasty! She wished she could have some more.

Later, Ann sneaked back into the kitchen. She took four more cookies! Now Ann feels sick. Her tummy hurts!

Ann made a bad choice. She ate too many cookies! Ann wants to make better choices. She asked Jesus to help her.

Jesus cares about what we eat. He wants us to be healthy. He can help you make good choices, too!

THINK: What are some foods that we should not eat often?

PRAYER: Dear Jesus, Please help me to choose good foods today. Amen.

9. Better than Food

IN MY BIBLE: *Then Jesus said, "I am the bread of life..."* ***John 6:35***

CHAT TIME

What if you did not eat all day? How would you feel? What if you did not eat for two days? You would be very hungry! We need food to be strong. We need food to grow. We need food to live!

There is something else we need. We need it even more than food. We need Jesus! Jesus tells us that He is the "Bread of Life." Just like we need food, we need to talk to Jesus. We need to read what He says in the Bible. Jesus is better than food!

DO: Draw a big loaf of bread. Write "JESUS" on it.

PRAYER: Dear Jesus, Thank You for food. And thank You for Your word. Amen.

10. More Water, Please

IN MY BIBLE: *He broke open a rock, and streams of water poured out.* ***Psalm 105:41***

CHAT TIME

It was bath time. Carl was dirty. He had played in the mud.

Carl filled a cup with water. He poured it into the bath tub. Then he got into the tub. He tried to take a bath. But he did not add any more water.

Do you think Carl got clean? No. We need a lot more water for a bath. One cup of water will not get us clean.

We need lots of water inside our bodies, too. Water helps to clean our bodies on the inside. We need to drink at least six glasses of water each day.

In the Bible, God gave good water to His people to drink. God wants us to drink lots of water, too. He wants us to be healthy.

THINK: What do we use water for each day?

PRAYER: Dear Jesus, Thank you for giving me clean water to drink each day. Amen.

11. Sweet Dreams

IN MY BIBLE: I will lie down and sleep in peace. Lord, you alone keep me safe. **Psalm 4:8**

CHAT TIME

"I don't want to go to bed. Why can't I stay up late?" Mark fussed. He wanted to keep playing.

"Our bodies need rest," Mom answered. "Our minds need rest, too. God made them that way. Sleep helps to keep us from getting sick. Sleep helps kids to grow. Without sleep, you cannot learn as well at school. You will not be as strong."

Mark still did not feel like sleeping. But he wanted to be strong to play ball at recess. He had lots of fun things to do the next day. He did not want to be tired or sick.

"I guess tomorrow will be better if I go to sleep tonight," Mark thought. Mark was right.

THINK: What do you like to do at bedtime?

PRAYER: Dear Jesus, Thank you for keeping me safe while I sleep. Amen.

12. Keep Moving!

IN MY BIBLE: ... His strength will last as long as he lives. **Deuteronomy 33:25**

CHAT TIME

What makes your body move? Muscles do! How many muscles you have? There are more than 600 muscles in your body. That is a lot! Some are in your arms and legs. Some are in your head and neck. Some are in your back and chest. Some are deep inside you. God made these muscles so we can move in lots of ways. We want to use our muscles a lot. It helps to keep them strong.

Some people do not use their muscles much. We should run and jump and climb. It helps our muscles to get stronger. Then we can do lots of things!

DO: Run or jump now to exercise your muscles.

PRAYER: Dear Jesus, Thank you for making me strong. Amen.

PART FOUR
Think Time

1. What Would Jesus Think?

2. The Storm

3. No Trash Here

4. Choose Joy

5. My Helper

6. In My Heart

7. What's On Your Mind?

8. Good Medicine

1. What Would Jesus Think?

IN MY BIBLE: *You should think in the same way Christ Jesus does.* ***Philippians 2:5***

CHAT TIME

Lynn and Kate were best friends. They talked a lot. They liked the same games at recess. They sat side by side at church.

Sometimes, Lynn would start to say something. Then Kate would finish Lynn's sentence. It seemed like they each knew what the other was thinking!

Jesus wants us to be really close to Him. He wants to be our best friend. He wants us to talk to Him a lot. He wants us to read His Word, the Bible. Then we will start to think the way that Jesus does. We can make the choices He wants us to make.

DO: Write a short note to your Best Friend, Jesus.

PRAYER: Dear Jesus, I am so glad that we are best friends. Thank you for loving me so much. Amen.

2. The Storm

IN MY BIBLE: *When I'm afraid, I will trust in you. Psalm 56:3*

CHAT TIME

There was a loud crash of thunder. It woke Rick up! Rick opened his eyes. He heard the rain outside. "Oh, no!" Rick thought. "A storm!"

Rick pulled the covers over his head. He shut his eyes tightly. Storms scared him.

"Rick?" It was Mom's voice. "Did the storm wake you up?"

"Yes," Rick said softly. "I am scared."

Mom sat on Rick's bed. They prayed and asked Jesus to keep them safe. They asked Jesus to help

Rick know that Jesus was with Him. Rick chose to let Jesus take away his fear. Rick thought about the angels around him. He fell asleep.

DO: Draw a picture of you with your angel beside you.

PRAYER: Dear Jesus, please help me to remember that You are always with me. Amen.

3. No Trash Here

IN MY BIBLE: *...always think about what is true. Think about what is noble, right and pure.* ***Philippians 4:7, 8***

CHAT TIME

"Look, Mom," Kay said. "A raccoon is at the trash can."

Mom looked outside. "You are right," she said. "I guess he is having some lunch."

"I am glad I do not get my lunch from a trash can." Kay made a face. "That would be gross."

Most boys and girls would not eat trash. But sometimes we put trash into our minds.

God says to think about things that are true, pure, and good. But at times, we choose to listen to lies. Our music or TV shows may not be good. That is like putting trash into our minds.

God wants to help us choose what to listen to. He can help us choose what to read and watch on TV. He will help us to put only good things into our minds.

DO: Draw a trash can. On it, write the words "lies" and "ugly words".

PRAYER: Dear Jesus, Please help me to think about good things. Amen

4. Choose Joy

IN MY BIBLE: *You will fill me with joy when I am with you.* **Psalm 16:11**

CHAT TIME

Jon woke up in a bad mood. He whined when he had to brush his teeth. He yelled at his sister. He fussed at breakfast. He pouted all the way to school.

"Jon," Dad said as they left for school. "You have a choice. You can choose to whine and make yourself and others sad. Or you can choose to smile and be nice to others. It is up to you. Why don't you let Jesus help you to be joyful?"

Each day, boys and girls have a choice, too. Jesus loves us. We can choose to let Him help us to be happy.

DO: Draw a picture of a happy face. Think of things that God has given you.

PRAYER: Dear Jesus, Please give me Your joy today. Amen.

5. My Helper

IN MY BIBLE: If any of you need wisdom, ask God for it. He will give it to you. **James 1:5**

CHAT TIME

"I can't do it!" Kayla sobbed. "I can't add these big numbers!"

"I know that you have worked hard," Mom said. She put her arm around Kayla. "Have you asked Jesus to help?"

"Does Jesus care about my math?" Kayla was not so sure.

"The Bible says that if we need wisdom, we should ask God. He can help us to learn things," Mom said.

"Then let us ask Him," said Kayla.

Kayla and Mommy talked to Jesus. They asked Him to help Kayla. They had a quick snack. Then they got all the math done!

What do you need help with? Don't forget to ask Jesus. He is just waiting to help you.

DO: Draw a picture of yourself doing something hard. Draw Jesus beside you, helping you.

PRAYER: Dear Jesus, I need Your help with _____. (Say what you need help with.) Please help me. Amen.

6. In My Heart

IN MY BIBLE: I have hidden your word in my heart so that I won't sin against you. **Psalm 119:11**

CHAT TIME

"Dad," Jack said one evening at supper. "Today Ray got so mad at me. He could not find his red toy sports car. He said that I took it. He yelled at me to give it back."

"Oh, no," Dad answered. "What did you do?"

"Well," said Jack. "I thought of a Bible verse. 'A gentle answer turns anger away.' So I asked Jesus to help me. I told Ray in a soft voice that I did not take his car."

"I helped Ray look for the car," said Jack. "We found it under Ray's bed. Ray told me that he was sorry he got mad at me."

"I am glad that you thought of your Bible verse," Dad said. "It is good to have God's word in our minds. It helps us to make good choices."

DO: Cut a big heart shape out of paper. Write the words "God's Word" on it.

PRAYER: Dear Jesus, Please help me to remember your Word. Amen.

7. What's on Your Mind?

IN MY BIBLE: Be careful what you think, because your thoughts run your life. **Proverbs 4:23**

CHAT TIME

Sam sat in his room. He was mad at his brother, Jake. Jake had used Sam's new book without asking. Sam had lots of angry thoughts about Jake. He thought about hurting Jake.

Sam came out of his room. Jake was in his way. He pushed Jake hard, and Jake fell. Jake cried.

Sam was sorry. He did not plan to hurt Jake. But when he saw Jake, Sam's angry thoughts came back. He told Mom all about it.

"Sam," Mom said kindly. "The Bible tells us that our thoughts affect what we do. Loving thoughts help us to be kind. Angry thoughts can lead us to hurt others."

Sam thought about what Mom said. He asked God to help him to choose good thoughts. Then he asked Jake to forgive him.

DO: Make a list of some nice things that you will do for someone today.

PRAYER: Dear Jesus, Please help me to think good thoughts today. Amen.

8. Good Medicine

IN MY BIBLE: *A happy heart is like good medicine...*
Proverbs 17:22

CHAT TIME

Have you ever been very sick? Did you have to take medicine? It may taste bad. We may have to get it in a shot with a needle. It can hurt! God tells us about a medicine that is fun. It is a "happy heart." God wants us to think glad thoughts. Glad thoughts can help us to stay well. Our minds can help our bodies.

We can think about nice things. We can think about fun times. We can think about good friends. We can think about our Friend, Jesus. We can think about Heaven.

God has given us many good things. We can have lots of happy thoughts. Then we can have better bodies, too!

DO: Draw pictures of two things that make you happy.

PRAYER: Dear Jesus, Thank you for all your good gifts. They give me lots of happy thoughts. Amen.

PART FIVE

Together Time

1. Helping

2. Playtime

3. About Obeying

4. A Thing Called Respect

5. Our words

6. Who Is That Bully?—1

7. Who Is That Bully?—2

8. Who Is That Bully?— 3

9. I Can Be Kind

10. I'm Special. You're Special.

11. Stop That Fight!

12. Love One Another

1. Helping

IN MY BIBLE: *Help each other with your troubles.*
Galatians 6:2

CHAT TIME

It was time for dinner, but the food was not on the table. Toby found Mother in bed.

"My head hurts," said Mother. "Will you please help me?"

Toby helped set the table. Then he helped Mother put the bread, some plums, and the bowls of soup on the table. Soon dinner was ready.

"Thank you, Toby, for your help," said Mother.

Toby was happy that he could help. Our Bible verse tells us that we must help others. We can help our little brothers and sisters. We can help older persons carry their packages. We can help our teachers. Will you help someone today?

DO: Make a list of things you could do to help somebody today.

PRAYER: Dear Jesus, I would like to help persons. Amen.

2. Playtime

IN MY BIBLE: *Two people are better than one. Ecclesiastes 4:9.*

CHAT TIME

Gabe and Ivan were playing with their bat and ball. Sometimes Gabe would throw the ball, and sometimes Ivan would throw the ball. Gabe liked it better when he was batting. So he started keeping his bat. Ivan had to throw the ball a lot.

"Please, Gabe, could I have the bat, too?" begged Ivan.

Still Gabe would not give Ivan a chance at the bat. Gabe took his bat and ball and went home. Soon Gabe found out that playing alone was not fun.

When we play with our friends, we must remember to share our toys and to take turns. When our friends win we must be happy for them. If we do not win, that is OK, too. Our Bible verse says that two are better than one. Have fun with your friends today.

THINK: Do you find it hard to be happy when your friends win?

PRAYER: Dear Jesus, please help me to be a good friend when I play. Amen.

3. About Obeying

IN MY BIBLE: *Children obey your parents the way the Lord wants.* **Ephesians 6:1**

CHAT TIME

Has your mom or dad or teacher ever had to tell you over and over to do something? There are some boys and girls who have to be told to do something over and over and over. They do not obey.

When we do what we are told to do, we are obeying. Jesus likes us to obey right away. Here are some ways to help us obey:

Come as soon as Mom or Dad calls us.
Find out what Mom or Dad wants us to do.
Do it right away.

Try it. You will like it. And Jesus will be happy.

THINK: What are some things that may keep you from obeying right away?

PRAYER: Dear Jesus, I want to obey. Please help me. Amen.

4. A Thing Called Respect

IN MY BIBLE: *When you talk you should always be kind and wise. Then you will be able to answer everyone in the way you should.* ***Colossians 4:6***

CHAT TIME

When we use a kind voice, and when we do kind things, especially to older persons, we show respect. We should also use a kind voice when we speak to our younger brothers and sisters and other kids. Everybody should get respect.

We can give our seat to an older person. We must not push an older person out of the way. We must say, "Excuse me," "I am sorry," "Thank you,"

"Please." We must wait our turn when someone else is speaking. When we show respect, Jesus is happy.

DO: See how many persons you can show respect to today.

PRAYER: Dear Jesus, Please help me to say and do kind things. Amen.

5. Our Words

IN MY BIBLE: *The right word spoken at the right time is as beautiful as gold apples in a silver bowl.* **Proverbs 25:11**

CHAT TIME

Sammy was mean. He liked to call people names. Elvis missed the ball. "Miss-the-ball-Elvis, you can do better than that," yelled Sammy.

Katie slipped and fell. "Cheers for Slippery Katie." Sammy clapped. Poor Katie started to cry in front of all of the kids.

"Stop saying those mean things!" Mr. Dole, the teacher, had just come into the room. "When we call persons names, it hurts. When we tell them things that are not kind, it hurts. Who would like to do better from now on?" asked Mr. Dole.

All hands went up. This class wanted to be as nice as that silver bowl in our Bible verse.

DO: Draw a big bowl of golden apples. Write some kind words on the apples.

PRAYER: Dear Jesus, please help me to use kind words today. Amen.

6. Who Is that Bully? –1

IN MY BIBLE: . . . *Defend the rights of the poor and needy. Proverbs 31:9*

CHAT TIME:

"RUN! KEEP RUNNING!" Big Joe was chasing after little Jim. Big Joe chased Jim all around the play field for the third time.

Poor Jim was scared. Jim was tired. "Please, please. I – I can't," cried Jim falling to the ground.

Big Joe stood there laughing. Joe was a bully. A bully is one who likes to hurt people. We can ask Jesus to help us not to be bullies.

Do: Draw a picture of Big Joe and Jim.

PRAYER: Dear Jesus, I do not want to be a bully. Amen

7. Who Is that Bully—2

IN MY BIBLE: . . . *A friend loves you all the time.* **Proverbs 17:17**

CHAT TIME:

Kathy and Mary stood chatting. "Look who is coming," said Mary.

Soon Sandy came closer to them. "Hi," said Sandy.

Kathy and Mary moved away.

"Hi, Kathy. Hi, Mary," said Sandy, as she ran to catch up with them.

"We do not want to play with you. That's all." Then Kathy and Mary ran to the other end of the playground.

Poor Sandy! There were tears in her eyes. *Why do they not want to play with me?*

A bully is one who pushes you out of the crowd to make you feel lonely. A bully does not want others to play with you. We can tell Jesus about the bully.

DO: Draw a picture of Kathy, Mary and Sandy.

PRAYER: Dear Jesus, please help me know that You will always be my friend. Amen.

8. Who Is that Bully—3

IN MY BIBLE: A *good person stays away from evil.* *Proverbs 16:17*

CHAT TIME:

Big Joe, Kathy and Mary are all bullies. A bully is one who tries to hurt us or make us feel sad. A bully may beat up on a weaker person. A bully may not want his or her friends to play with you. A bully just likes to make you feel very bad and very sad.

We must keep away from anyone who is a bully. Read today's Bible verse.

DO: Put an X beside each statement if you think that person is a bully:

Likes to hurt, hit and scare persons who

are smaller and weaker ( )

Tells his or her friends not to play with

a person ( )

Starts fights between others ( )

Takes away persons' toys, lunch, etc. ( )

Always tell an adult when a bully hurts you or says that he or she will hurt you.

PRAYER: Dear Jesus, please take care of me. AMEN

9. I Can Be Kind

IN MY BIBLE: Be kind and loving to each other.
Ephesians 4:32

CHAT TIME:

"Give it to me. It is MINE!" cried little Tommy.

"You have to catch me first," said big sister Jenny, as she ran from her brother's room.

"What is going on?" asked Mother hanging up the phone. Mother found out the whole story. Jenny took away Tommy's box of crayons.

"Jesus likes us to be kind to everyone," said Mother. Can we try that today?" said Mother. "Why don't we have a Kindness Day, today?"

"A kindness day!" said both children. "What's that?"

"Well, today we will be kind to everyone in this house. Even Rover. Our dog, Rover would like some kindness, too, you know," said Mother smiling.

So for the whole day, that house was full of kindness. Even Rover liked it.

DO: Would you like to have a Kindness Day at your house? Write down some of the things you would do on your Kindness Day.

PRAYER: Dear Jesus, Please help me to be kind today and always. Amen.

10. I'm Special. You're Special

IN MY BIBLE: But Christ died for us while we were still sinners. In this way God showed His great love for us. **Romans 5:8**

CHAT TIME

"Mom," said Sara at bedtime, "My friends don't think I am special. Nobody does."

"I really think you are, Sara, and I hope *you* think so too," said Mother. "That matters a lot, you know. You are also special because God made you. He loves you. Jesus died for you. Mommy, Daddy, Grandma, and some other people love you a lot. Now, aren't you really special?" Mom asked.

"I guess so," said Sara with a big smile and hugging Mother.

DO: Write on a paper, "I am special." Hang it over your bed.

PRAYER: Thank you, Jesus, for making me special. Amen.

11. Stop that Fight!

IN MY BIBLE: *So stop the quarrel before a fight breaks out.* ***Proverbs 17:14***

CHAT TIME

Have you ever wondered how a fight starts? It often starts with words. People yell angry words at each other. We call that a quarrel. Some boys and girls hit each other. Some persons like to fight. That is not a good idea.

But what if a quarrel starts anyway? Well, we say to our friend, "Why don't we talk about this thing quietly? I will listen to you, and then you can listen to me." Then try talking with soft voices. Perhaps the person will not want to fight anymore.

That sounds like a good idea, does it not? So today there will be no quarrels and no fights.

DO: Stand in front of the mirror and say, "I will not shout or yell today."

PRAYER: Dear Jesus, please help me to be a peace-maker. Amen.

12. Love One Another

IN MY BIBLE: *The greatest of these is love. I Corinthians 13:13*

CHAT TIME

Nancy said, "Mom, I love you." But Nancy hated to help her mom in the house.

Toby told his little brother, "I love you." But Toby would not play with him. Little Brother was sad and lonely. Little Brother cried.

Did Nancy and Toby really love? Perhaps they did. But they did not do things to show that they loved.

Jesus says that when we love, we show it. Let us love some more today. Can we show it?

DO: Write some things you can do to show love.

PRAYER: Dear Jesus, please help me to love. Amen.

PART SIX
Story Time with Jesus

1. The Peacemakers

2. When Someone Is Sorry — 1

3. When Someone Is Sorry — 2

4. Smart Guy, Silly Guy

5. The Wedding

1. The Peacemakers

IN MY BIBLE: *Those who work to bring peace are happy. **Matthew 5:9***

CHAT TIME

Mike and Megan had been fighting for most of the day.

"Can't you two just get along?" asked Mother. "We need a plan for peace."

"Peace!" said Mike. "What is peace?"

"Well," said Mother. "Peace means that there is no fighting and yelling. Peace means that we use kind words. Peace means that we speak in kind voices."

"What if Mike yells at me?" asked Megan. "How can there be no fighting?"

"When things do not go right," said Mother, "We will say, 'Let's work it out.' Jesus says that people who make peace will be happy. Can you try that?"

"I – I – think so," said Megan.

"OK, PEACEMAKERS' DAY. Let's work it out," said Mike.

DO: Read today's Bible verse again.

PRAYER: Dear Jesus, please help me to be a peace-maker. Amen.

2. When Someone Is Sorry — 1

IN MY BIBLE: *Yes, if you forgive others for the things they do wrong, then your Father in heaven will also forgive you for the things you do wrong.* ***Matthew 6:14***

CHAT TIME:

Jesus told a story about a servant who borrowed thousands of dollars from the king. The poor servant could not pay the money back.

"You must sell your tables and chairs. You must even sell your wife and children. That will give you the money to pay me back," said the angry king.

"Oh no, please, I will work hard to pay you back," begged the servant.

The king felt sorry for the servant. "OK, you do not have to pay me."

"Oh, thank you," cried the man. "Thank you." The servant was very happy.

DO: Draw a picture of the servant begging the king to help him.

PRAYER: Dear Jesus, please give me a kind heart. Amen.

3. When Someone Is Sorry — 2

IN MY BIBLE: *But if you don't forgive the wrongs of others, then your Father in heaven will not forgive the wrong things you do.* ***Matthew 6:15***

CHAT TIME

A poor servant owed the king thousands of dollars. The kind king did not sent him to jail for his money. One day, that poor servant met another servant who owed him just a few dollars."Hey," said the first servant to a man who had money for him. "I want my money now; or you will go to jail!

The other servant begged and cried. But that bad servant sent him to jail.

"King, that servant you were so kind to, put a man who owed him money in jail," said someone to the king one day.

"Really!" said the king. "Well, I will send him to jail for my money, too."

Jesus always forgives us for the wrong things we do. So we must also forgive people who do us wrong things. Jesus would like that.

DO: What do you need to do to forgive somebody?

PRAYER: Dear Jesus, please help me forgive people who do me wrong. Amen.

4. Smart Guy, Silly Guy

IN MY BIBLE: *But the house did not fall, because the house was built on rock.* ***Matthew 7:25***

CHAT TIME

Once there was a smart man who built a new house. This smart man build his house on rock. The house was strong. A big storm came with lots of winds and rain. The house did not fall down.

Then there was a silly man. He built his nice new house on the sand. Along came a big storm with lots of rain. The sand got wet and loose. So the house fell.

People, who read their Bibles, and do what Jesus says, are like that smart man with the strong house. People, who do not read their Bibles and do not do what Jesus says, are silly. Do you want to be like the wise man? Follow Jesus.

DO: Draw a picture of some guys doing silly things.

PRAYER: Dear Jesus, please help me to listen to You. I want to be wise. Amen.

5. The Wedding

IN MY BIBLE: *So always be ready. You don't know the day or the time the Son of Man will come.* ***Matthew 25:13***

CHAT TIME

Ten beautiful girls were going to march in a wedding. They were going to march with lamps in their hands. In those days people put oil in their lamps, to give them light. Well, the groom was late. So the ten girls took a nap.

Suddenly, someone said, "The groom is coming! It's time for the wedding! Girls, it is time to march in the wedding! Get your lamps!"

The girls woke up. Some lamps had no light! Oh no! Only five of the girls had oil in their lamps. So only these five girls could be in the wedding because they had lighted lamps! The other five girls ran to the store to buy oil. But they missed the wedding. They were very sad.

Jesus is coming back to earth. We do not know when, but we must always be ready. We must be thinking about Jesus. We must read our Bibles to know what Jesus wants us to do. We must not be like those girls who were not ready. We do not want to miss being with Jesus. We want to be ready.

Do: Draw some persons getting ready for a wedding.
PRAYER: Dear Jesus, please help me to be ready to meet You. Amen.

PART SEVEN

Promise Time

1. Always Able

2. Here Comes Joy

3. Don't Be Afraid

4. You Can Finish It

5. My Guide

6. He Will Answer

7. Just Ask

8. My Body Guard

9. Don't Worry

10. I Will Come Again

1. Always Able

IN MY BIBLE: Is anything too hard for the Lord? **Genesis 18:14**

CHAT TIME

Susie was mad at everybody. Then Susie started crying. Susie was really sad, too. Poor Susie!

"What's the matter, Susie?" asked Mother. "You have not been yourself this afternoon."

"Oh, Mother. This room is so messy. I need to clean my room. I do not even know where to begin. Mother, I can't. I know I can't." Susie cried even more.

"Never mind," said Mother in a soft voice. "You are going to be OK. First we will pray to Jesus to help us. There is nothing too hard for Jesus," said Mother. "Jesus is always able."

Susie slowly dried her tears. She and Mother prayed. Then, she and Mother looked at all the things they had to do. Bit by bit, they worked together. Then they finished cleaning. Mother and Susie were happy.

DO: Make a poster that says JESUS IS ALWAYS ABLE

PRAYER: Dear Jesus, I am so glad You can do anything. Amen.

2. Here Comes Joy

IN MY BIBLE: Crying may last for a night. But joy comes in the morning. **Psalm 30:5**

CHAT TIME

Last night Ron did not sleep well. Ron's mom was sick. But that was not all. Dad did not have a job anymore. What was going to happen now? Things were bad.

Sometimes things get bad. Sometimes we do not know when things will get better. Just remember our Bible verse. We may be sad, but only for a while. Jesus will help us get over the bad times. Joy will come again because Jesus cares.

DO: Draw a picture of a sunrise.

PRAYER: Dear Jesus, Please help me remember that You care about me. Amen.

3. Don't Be Afraid

IN MY BIBLE: Don't be afraid, because I am your God. **Isaiah 41:10**

CHAT TIME

Mother tucked Anita into bed, Anita started to cry. "Mother, please come."

Mother ran to Anita's room.. "Anita, Is everything all right?"

"Mother, I am so afraid. What's that sound?" asked Anita.

"Oh, that is the clock ticking," replied Mother. TICK TOCK went the clock.. "Anita," said Mother gently. "Jesus tells us in the Bible not to be afraid. Jesus will take care of us. So, when you are afraid say, 'Jesus, I am afraid. Please help me.' Then sing a little song." Mother kissed Anita and left the room.

A few minutes later, Mother heard Anita humming softly.

DO: Pick a song you could sing when you are afraid.
PRAYER: Dear Jesus, please help me to remember that you are with me. I will not be afraid. Amen.

4. You Can Finish It

IN MY BIBLE: God began doing a good work in you. And He will continue it until it is finished . . . **Philippians 1:6**

CHAT TIME

Ted took his plate to the kitchen. There was a half-eaten banana on the plate. There was also half a slice of toast. Ted had not drunk all of his milk.

"Oh no!" said Mother, feeling sad. She was holding Ted's homework paper. Ted did not finish his homework. Ted did not even take his homework to school!

"Ted, we have to help you finish what you have started," Mother told Ted after school. "We must not just start things. We must finish them too."

Mother and Ted prayed that Jesus would help Ted to start and finish things. Jesus helped Ted.

THINK: Are there some things you have started and not finished? Your homework? Your piano lesson? Something you promised to help Mother with? Jesus can help you.

PRAYER: Dear Jesus, please help me to finish what I have started. Amen.

5. My Guide

IN MY BIBLE: . . . *I will guide you and watch over you. Psalm 32:8*

CHAT TIME

What does this Bible verse mean? It means that Jesus is watching over us. He will be with us always.

A blind man went to the store. It was a big store. The blind man was buying things. He had a big dog guiding him. Some dogs can guide people who are blind. These dogs are called "seeing eye dogs." They are also called "guide dogs."

Jesus guides us too. He sees everything. He is the best guide a kid could have. You can trust Him.

DO: Draw a man with his guide dog.

PRAYER: Dear Jesus, please guide me today. Amen

6. He Will Answer

IN MY BIBLE: Call unto me and I will answer thee. . .
Jeremiah 33:3

CHAT TIME

The phone rang five times. There was no answer. Grandma was at the airport. No one was there to meet her. Grandma waited.

"Hi, Grandma! Hi, Grandma!" Judy and Jenny ran towards Grandma.

"Oh, it is so good to see you!" said Grandma kissing the girls. "I tried calling you but - - -"

"Well, we were on our way to meet you," said Mr. Jones, Grandma's son. Mr. Jones was Judy and Jenny's dad. "I am so glad to see you, Mom." He, too, hugged Grandma.

Jesus tells us to call Him. He is always there to take our call. And He will answer us, too. That is great!

DO: Draw a big phone.

PRAYER: Dear Jesus, thank You for hearing my prayers. Amen.

7. Just Ask

IN MY BIBLE: Continue to ask God and God will give to you. **Matthew 7:7**

CHAT TIME

"What are you doing, Jack?" asked Betty.

"It is my wish list," said Jack. "It is a list of things I would like for my birthday."

"All of those things? Seems like a pretty long list to me," said Betty, Jack's older sister. "I hope you get your wishes."

"Well, at least I will ask Mom and Dad," said Jack.

Today's Bible verse is a promise from Jesus. We have a Father in heaven whom we can ask for things. Jesus says that when we want something we can ask Him.

THINK: Have you ever asked Jesus for anything?

PRAYER: Dear Jesus, I am glad you hear my prayers. Amen.

8. My Body Guard

IN MY BIBLE: *God is our protection and our strength. Psalm 46:1*

CHAT TIME

A body guard is one who walks around with impor- tant persons to be sure that they are safe. Body guards do not let anybody hurt those persons.

Kings and queens have body guards. Presidents have body guards. When people go to the bank with a lot of money, they sometimes have body guards.

Did you know that you, too, have a body guard? Take a look at today's Bible verse. That's right. God is your body guard. He will take care of you. He will keep you safe. Don't forget this.

DO: Draw a picture of you with a body guard.

PRAYER: Dear Jesus I am glad You will keep me safe. Amen.

9. Don't Worry

IN MY BIBLE: Give your worries to the Lord. He will take care of you. **Psalm 55:22**

CHAT TIME

Jan sat with her pencil and paper in her hand. "I cannot draw," said Jan. Jan drew her picture. Then she hid it in her desk. "I do not want anyone to see it." Jan worried about what her teacher would say about her drawing.

Soon the teacher came by. "Let us have a look, Jan. Nice job."

Jan smiled. That was not so bad.

Sometimes we worry about our homework. Sometimes we worry that our friends may not like us. Jesus does not want us to worry. He can help us. Don't worry.

THINK: What are some things you worry about?

PRAYER: Dear Jesus, please help me not to worry. Amen.

10. I Will Come Again

IN MY BIBLE: . . . *I will come back*. **John 14:3**

CHAT TIME

Chuck saw Sam's parents put many boxes into the van. Sam and his parents were moving. They were going to live very far from Chuck. That made Chuck very sad.

"Bye, Chuck," Sam said. "I am going to miss you."

"Are you going to come back to see me?" asked Chuck. He was beginning to think he would cry.

"Well, maybe." Sam was not too sure.

One day Jesus told his friends on earth that He was going away. His friends were very sad. They loved Jesus. They were going to miss him.

Then Jesus said that He would come back to earth. That is true. Jesus is coming back. When He comes back, He will take us with Him to heaven. Let us keep waiting for Him.

DO: Draw a picture of Jesus coming back to earth.

PRAYER: Dear Jesus, please come back soon. Amen.

PART EIGHT
BIBLE Story Time

1. When the Whole World Got Sad

2. No, Thank You

3. Sorry, You Can't Go with Them—1

4. Sorry, You Can't Go with Them —2

5. The King who Disobeyed

6. The Boy Who Did Not Listen

1. When the Whole World Got Sad

IN MY BIBLE*: ". . . but of the tree of the knowledge of good and evil, you shall not eat." **Gen. 2: 17***

CHAT TIME

A long time ago, Adam and Eve did not obey God in the Garden of Eden. So this world became full of sadness? There is pain and sickness now.

Sometimes moms and dads and other adults do not obey God. Grown-ups need to obey Jesus, too. Some boys and girls do not obey their parents. Or they may take a long time before they obey. This makes Jesus very sad.

We all must obey Jesus. He knows what is best for us.

THINK: When was the last time you did not obey? You can talk to Jesus about it.

PRAYER: Dear Jesus, please help me to obey. Amen.

2. No, Thank You

IN MY BIBLE: . . . *but for Cain and his offering He had no regard. **Gen. 4**: 5*

CHAT TIME:

Cain and Abel were two brothers. Cain was a farmer. He planted fruits and vegetables. Abel was a shepherd. He took care of sheep and lambs. One day God asked Cain and Abel to take Him a lamb each.

Cain took God some fruits and vegetables. God did not like what Cain did. God was very sad and said, "No, thank you, Cain." Abel obeyed and took God a lamb. God was happy to take the lamb from Abel. God likes us to be obedient.

DO: Draw a sad face and a happy face.

PRAYER: Dear Jesus, I do not want to make You sad. Please help me to always obey You. Amen.

3. Sorry, You Can't Go with Them—1

IN MY BIBLE: . . . *"Speak ye unto the rock." **Numbers 20: 8***

CHAT TIME:

Moses and his brother, Aaron, were leaders of many people called Israelites. They all lived in the hot desert. The people were very thirsty and there was no water. They kept asking Moses and Aaron for water.

"God, we have no water," said Moses. "What shall we do?"

God told Moses to go to a rock and speak to it. Then water will come out of that rock. Moses and the people went to the rock. "Why are we here?' said some of the people. "Moses, we need water."

Moses became angry. He did not speak to the rock. Moses hit the rock twice, with a big stick that was in his hand. Soon, there was a lot of water all around. All of the people were able to drink lots of water.

DO: Draw a picture of today's story.

PRAYER: Dear God, please let me always do what You tell me to do. Amen.

4. Sorry, You Can't Go with Them −2

IN MY BIBLE: *Obey me . . . and good things will happen to you. **Jeremiah 7:23***

CHAT TIME:

In our last story, we saw that God told Moses to speak to the rock and water would come. Moses did not obey. He hit the rock twice. God was very sad.

"Moses," said God. I was going to take you to a very nice country called Canaan. But you did not obey me. I told you to speak to the rock. But you hit it. I am sorry, Moses. You cannot go to Canaan. The other people may go."

Moses was very sad. When we do not obey, bad things happen.

THINK: Can you remember a bad thing that happened to you or anyone else who did not obey?

PRAYER: Please help me, Jesus, to obey always. Amen.

5. The King Who Disobeyed

IN MY BIBLE: Behold, to obey is better than sacrifice. **1 Samuel 15:22**

CHAT TIME:

Once there was a king called Saul. Men from his country and another country were fighting. The people from the other country got scared and ran away. They left a lot of clothes, sheep and money behind. God told King Saul to throw all of that stuff away. King Saul looked at the money and the sheep and the clothes. Then the king said, "Maybe I could give these nice fat sheep to God."

That was a bad plan. God did not want those things from King Saul. Why did King Saul not obey God? Sometimes we do what **we** want to do. Our

Bible tells us that it is always better to obey God. Let us always remember that.

THINK: What are some ways that people disobey God?

PRAYER: Jesus, please help me listen to You and do what you tell me. Amen.

6. The Boy Who Did Not Listen

IN MY BIBLE: My child, listen to your father's teaching. **Proverbs 1.8**

CHAT TIME:

Samson was big and very strong. He killed a lion one day. One day Samson saw a pretty girl. He told his mom and dad that he wanted to marry her.

"No, please do not marry her," said his mom and dad. "She does not love God. We wish you would marry a girl who loves God."

Samson would not listen to his parents. He married that girl. Samson had many friends who did not love God; and they did not love Samson either. One day they put Samson in jail and he died there. If only Samson had obeyed his parents.

DO: Draw a picture of Samson's mom and dad.

PRAYER: Dear Jesus, please help me to obey my parents and Your Word.

PART NINE

A Time for Good Habits

1. Cheerfulness

2. Joy

3. Friendliness

4. Good Job

5. Keeping at It

6. Learning

7. Sharing My Faith

8. No Boasting Here

9. Patience

10. Hope

11. Honesty

12. Giving to Others

1. Cheerfulness

IN MY BIBLE: *A merry heart maketh a cheerful countenance.* **Proverbs 15:13**

CHAT TIME:

Lauren was doing her chores. Lauren hated chores. She would not smile. She was miserable. Mother said that Lauren's face was like a rainy day.

Sometimes persons do not smile because they are sad. They may be hurting inside. Then there are others who are not sad, but they like to pout. We look ugly when we pout.

We can become cheerful if we let Jesus into in our hearts. Then we will smile. People will smile back at us. Boys and girls who are cheerful feel better and look better. They make others feel better, too.

DO: See how many persons you can smile at today.

PRAYER: Jesus, please come into my heart and make me cheerful. Amen.

2. Joy

IN MY BIBLE: *. . . for the joy of the Lord is your strength.* ***Nehemiah 8:10***

CHAT TIME:

Have you ever been happy one day and sad the next day? We wish we could be happy all the time. Happiness does not last. That's too bad.

The Bible verse today talks about joy. When we love Jesus, there is joy. That joy from Jesus stays in our hearts and makes us happy. It lasts for a long,

long time. There is no other Person who can give us this joy. Only Jesus can. This is real joy.

THINK: What would this world be like if we all had the joy of Jesus in our hearts?

PRAYER: Dear Jesus, please put Your joy in my heart. Amen.

3. Friendliness

IN MY BIBLE: *A man that hath friends must shew himself friendly.* **Proverbs 18:24**

CHAT TIME:

The other kids were playing outside. Sandy did not go out to play.

"Come on, Sandy," invited Dan and Susie. "Let's play."

Sandy would not go. Sandy did not talk to the other kids much. Sandy was not friendly. Sandy had no friends. Then one day Sandy went outside with the other kids. "Dan, Susie, could I play with you?" asked Sandy.

Dan, Susie and Sandy played many games. They had a good time. Now Sandy had two friends. She felt better. Then she tried to get more friends.

THINK: Is it a good thing to have friends? How do you pick your friends?

PRAYER: Dear Jesus, please help me to be a good friend. Amen.

4. Good Job

IN MY BIBLE: *Whatever work you do, do your best.*
Ecclesiastes 9:10

CHAT TIME:

Mother watched as Megan swept the kitchen floor and pushed the dirt under the rug. Megan did not do a good job with the dishes, either. Mother was sad.

"Megan, you did not do a good job with the floor nor the dishes," said Mother. "When you have a job, you must always do your best."

Megan thought about that. She was going to do better from now on.

The next time you have a job to do, be sure to do it well. Do your best. You will feel good about yourself.

THINK: What would happen if we everybody in the world did not do a good job?

PRAYER: I would like to do my best always. Amen.

5. Keeping at It

IN MY BIBLE: *Do you see a man skilled in his work? That man will work for kings. He won't have to work for ordinary people.* **Proverbs 22:29**

CHAT TIME:

Jenny's eyes filled with tears. She got up from the piano. "It's no use," she said. "I cannot get my notes right."

"You have got to keep at it, Jenny," said Mrs. Loo, Jenny's piano teacher. "Keep at it all the time. You will find that bit by bit you will do better. "

The next day, Jenny was up early, and at the piano. Then after school, Jenny went to the piano again. By the next week, Jenny was playing very much better.

Is there something that you find very hard? Don't give up. Just keep at it. Jesus will help you, too.

DO: Make a list of some things you need to keep at.

PRAYER: Dear Jesus, with You I can do anything. Amen.

6. Learning

IN MY BIBLE: *Wisdom is more precious than rubies.* ***Proverbs 8:11***

CHAT TIME:

When he was a little boy, Sam did not like to go to school. So he did not learn to read. Sam grew up and he worked very hard. He still could not read. That was very sad.

Boys and girls need to go to school and study hard. Boys and girls need to learn as much as they can. The things you learn in school will help you when you grow up. You can become smart. Jesus has promised to help us if we ask Him.

THINK: What are some things you cannot do if you are not able to read?

PRAYER: Jesus, please make me wise. Amen.

7. Sharing My Faith

IN MY BIBLE: *You will be my witnesses . . . Acts 1:8.*

CHAT TIME:

Lena and Roland heard their teacher at church talk about sharing their faith. "When we help others meet Jesus, we are sharing our faith," said Teacher Brown. Lena and Roland asked Grandpa how they could share their faith.

"Yes, it is just telling others about Jesus. We are to be His witnesses. A witness tells what he or she knows about something or somebody. Well, what do you know about Jesus?" asked Grandpa.

"He loves us. He died to save us," said Lena.

"He will take us to heaven to be with Him," added Roland.

"So that's what you will tell your friends," said Grandpa smiling. "Also, you can be kind and loving like Jesus. When your friends look at you they will think of Jesus. They will want to be like Him. That is what sharing your faith is all about."

DO: Make a list of things boys and girls can do to be witnesses.

PRAYER: Dear Jesus, please help me to be Your witness. Amen.

8. No Boasting Here

IN MY BIBLE: *Pride leads only to shame.* ***Proverbs 11:2***

CHAT TIME:

Everybody was talking about the graduation dinner. "Nobody will have a dress like mine. I think I will look the best," Sarah told her sister, Minnie.

The evening of the dinner came. All eyes were on Sarah as she started walking to her seat. Then, oops! Sarah slipped and fell—right in front of everyone! Sarah started crying.

The kids said that Sarah had been boasting too much. We do not want to have pride in our hearts. That is what today's Bible verse says. Jesus could keep us from shame and pride.

THINK: Have you ever boasted?

PRAYER: Dear Jesus, please take away pride from my heart. Amen.

9. Patience

IN MY BIBLE: *Let your patience show itself perfectly in what you do. **James 1:4***

CHAT TIME:

Have you ever seen people in a hurry? They do not want to wait their turn. Some persons push their way to the front of the line. People who do not like to wait do not have patience.

The Bible tells us that it is a good thing to wait. We must learn to wait. That means we need to have patience. The Bible also tells us that people who have patience will get to heaven. We can ask Jesus to give us patience.

THINK: What are some things that people who do not have patience do?

PRAYER: Lord, please give me patience. Amen.

10. Hope

IN MY BIBLE: . . . *my hope is in thee.* ***Psalm 39:7***

CHAT TIME:

When we have hope we believe that good things will happen. If we do not have hope then we feel sad. Satan does not like us to have hope. He wants us to think that life is bad all the time.

Jesus is our hope. We have the hope that He will save us from our sins. We have the hope that He will take us to heaven with Him. So when we have Jesus in our hearts, we will have hope. People who do not know Jesus do not have hope. Even when things are really bad, the hope from Jesus will help us.

DO: Write some things that you are hoping for.

PRAYER: Thank You, Jesus for the hope You give us. Amen.

11. Honesty

IN MY BIBLE: *The good person who lives an honest life is a blessing to his children.* **Proverbs 20:7**

CHAT TIME:

"This CD is $10," the man at the cash register told Abe.

Abe gave the man a $20 bill. When Abe looked at his change, he could not believe his eyes. He had got $20 back! He should have got back $10. The man at the cash register had made a mistake. What was Abe to do? Abe talked to his Mom.

"What do you think you should do, Abe?" asked Mom.

Abe said he would take the money back to the store. He should have got back only $10. "I want to be honest, Mom." Mother took Abe to the store, and he gave back the $20. The man at the cash register gave him the right change.

Mom was proud of Abe. Abe felt good. Best of all, Jesus was happy to see another honest kid.

THINK: If you were Abe, what would you have done?

PRAYER: Dear Jesus, please help me to be honest. Amen.

12. Giving to Others

IN MY BIBLE: *Whenever you are able, do good to people who need help.* ***Proverbs 3:27.***

CHAT TIME:

"Please help the poor. Help the poor, please," said the man on the sidewalk.

Toby looked at the man. "Why is he asking for money, Dad?"

Dad told Toby that some poor people did not have homes or food or warm clothes. "God has blessed us with a home, good food and warm clothes. We can help these poor people. We can give money to help the homeless people, too."

Jesus is pleased when we give help to those who need it

DO: What are some things you and your friends can do to help poor persons?

PRAYER: Dear Jesus, please help us to be kind to the poor people. Amen.

PART TEN

Going Home Time:
Best Friends Forever

1. A Big City

2. A Wonderful City

3. Heaven Will Be Safe

4. No Night There

5. My Head Hurts

6. Here, Kitty Kitty

1. A Big City

IN MY BIBLE: *The city had a great high wall with 12 gates.* ***Revelation 21:12***

CHAT TIME:

Mike was doing his homework. "Mother, we have to find five big cities."

"Well, let us take a look at the map," said Mother.

Soon Mike had finished his homework.

"Mike," said Mother. "Did you know that heaven has a big city? The Bible says that it is a big square city. It is 1400 miles long, 1400 miles wide and 1400 miles high." (Revelation 21:16, *New International Reader's Version*).

Mike's eyes got wide. "That is a lot of space to play!" said Mike. "I think Heaven will be fun!"

Would you like to go there? Jesus wants you to be with Him.

DO: Take a map and see some of the big cities. Ask someone to help you.

PRAYER: Dear Jesus, thank you for the big city You made for us in heaven. Amen.

2. A Wonderful City

IN MY BIBLE: *It was shining bright like an expensive jewel, like jasper.* ***Revelation 21:11***

CHAT TIME:

Perhaps you have been into a store that sells jewels. Some stores have lots of shining jewels: diamonds, pearls, rubies, and other pretty stones. Heaven will be nicer than those stores.

The Bible says that the gates will be made of pearls; and there will be golden streets. Imagine running on golden streets! There is no place here on earth that has jewels stuck all over it.

Heaven is going to be wonderful. Jesus wants you there.

DO: Draw a pretty stone.

PRAYER: Dear Jesus, I want to go to heaven with You. Please help me. Amen.

3. Heaven Will Be Safe

IN MY BIBLE: *Only what is pure will enter it. Revelation 21: 27*

CHAT TIME

"Well, Boys and Girls, Officer Max will be talking to us today," said the teacher.

"Boys and Girls," said the cop in a big voice, "I am here to tell you that we want you to be safe. There are lots of rules to keep us safe." Officer Max held up a DVD. "Here are some of these rules:

Do not talk to strangers when you are alone.

We will not take food from persons when we are not with our parents or guardians.

We must always keep our doors locked.

I wish we did not need these rules," said Officer Max. "But we have to keep safe."

Our Bible tells us that in heaven, nothing will hurt or scare us. Heaven will be safe.

THINK: What are some other things kids should do to be safe?

PRAYER: Dear Jesus, please keep me safe. I am glad heaven will be safe. Amen.

4. No Night There

IN MY BIBLE: *There will never be night again.*
Revelation 22:5

CHAT TIME

Some kids are afraid of the dark. When Mom or Dad
or Grandma or Grandpa puts them to bed, they are
scared. Older persons are not afraid of the dark. It
is OK to go to bed at night.

Well, in heaven, no one will be afraid of the dark.
Light will always be there. Why? Well, there will be
no more night. Today's Bible verse says that. "There
will never be night again." That sounds like fun.

DO: Draw a picture of your bedtime.

PRAYER: Dear Jesus, thank you for making heaven such a special place. Amen.

5. My Head Hurts

IN MY BIBLE: . . . *There will be no more crying or pain. **Revelation 21:4***

CHAT TIME:

"Mommy, my head hurts," cried Tina. "Mommy!"

Mother rushed into Tina's room. Mother put her hand on Tina's cheek. "Oh, Tina. You have a fever. You are burning up. We will go to Doctor Kim."

Doctor Kim looked into Tina's throat. She looked at Tina's tongue. She looked into Tina's eyes. "Hmm. You are pretty sick, Tina. We will have you better soon." She gave some pills to Tina's mom. "Please give these to her and have her drink lots of water."

The next day, Tina felt better.

Sometimes when we get sick we have a lot of pain. When we get to Heaven, we will not get sick. We will not have pain.

DO: Draw a picture of Tina and the doctor.

PRAYER: Dear Jesus, please help the sick people to feel better. Amen.

6. Here, Kitty, Kitty

IN MY BIBLE: ... *Calves, lions and young bulls will eat together. And a little child will lead them.* **Isaiah 11:6**

CHAT TIME:

We love our pets. Don't we? We will have pets in heaven. We will be able to run and play with those big animals we are now afraid of. Yes, the animals will not hurt us.

Would you like to pat a fluffy lion? Would you like to go for a long ride on the back of a tall ostrich? You could fly on the wings of an eagle.

Heaven would be fun with all of those animals. Jesus wants you there.

THINK: Which animal would you like to play with in heaven?

PRAYER: Dear Jesus, thanks for the animals. I would like to go to heaven. Amen.

CPSIA information can be obtained at www.ICGtesting.com
Printed in the USA
LVOW092025290612

288109LV00002B/1/P

9 781613 797181